FRIENDSHIPS

by

Rob Long

A NASEN PUBLICATION

Published in 1999

© Rob Long

ISBN 1 901485 09 9

The right of Rob Long to be identified as author of this work has been asserted by him in accordance with the Copyright, Designs and Patents Act 1988.

Published by NASEN.
NASEN is a company limited by guarantee, registered in England and Wales. Company No. 2674379.
NASEN is a registered charity. Charity No. 1007023.

Further copies of this book and details of NASEN's many other publications may be obtained from the Publications Department at its registered office: NASEN House, 4/5 Amber Business Village, Amber Close, Amington, Tamworth, Staffs. B77 4RP.
Tel: 01827 311500; Fax: 01827 313005
Email: welcome@nasen.org.uk; Website: www.nasen.org.uk

Cover design by Raphael Creative Design.
Typeset in Times by J. C. Typesetting and printed in the United Kingdom by Stowes (Stoke-on-Trent).

Contents

Preface

Frienships is one of eight booklets in the series *Making Sense of Behaviour* by Rob Long. The others are *Exercising Self-control; Developing Self-esteem through Positive Entrapment for Pupils facing Emotional and Behavioural Difficulties; Understanding and Supporting Depressed Children and Young People; Not Me, Miss! The Truth about Children who Lie; Challenging Confrontation: Information and Techniques for School Staff; Supporting Pupils with Emotional and Behavioural Difficulties through Consistency;* and *Learning to Wave: Some Everyday Guidelines for Stress Management.*

The first five titles give practical ideas and information for teachers to use with children with worrying behaviours in their classes. These are written to help teachers both understand and change some of the difficulties that children might experience (depression, lack of self-control, low self-esteem, friendship problems and lying).

Challenging Confrontation gives information and techniques for teachers to use when dealing with argumentative, angry and difficult pupils. *Supporting Pupils with Emotional and Behavioural Difficulties through Consistency* advocates a whole-school approach for low-level misbehaviours whilst *Learning to Wave* is written for teachers themselves. It contains advice about coping with the stress which might arise from dealing with children with behavioural problems.

Each book stands alone but when read as a set the behavioural issues and their solutions overlap and this emphasises the need for positive and consistent strategies to be put into place throughout the school.

Acknowledgements
The author and publishers wish to express their grateful thanks to Lorna Johnston, Agnes Donnelly and Dorothy Smith for their helpful suggestions and comments.

Friendships

Introduction

Not all children find it easy to make friends. There are some who neither want or need friends. If a child is happy to play alone then there is no problem. But if they play alone because they do not have the skills or understanding of how to be a friend then that is a different matter. Most children are unhappy and miserable without friends; they experience feelings of loneliness, rejection and anger. Their behaviour will usually reflect these feelings, leading them to be more aggressive or to display symptoms of inadequacy. This booklet will consider some of the key aspects of friendship and then consider ways in which we can actively support children who face this challenge. Friendship skills are learnt skills and like any other skill can be taught.

This booklet is aimed at children and young people who experience friendship difficulties. It aims to provide information and understanding about friendships as well as ideas and strategies to enable schools to promote success and confidence through friendship. While some of the ideas may be helpful and applicable to children whose difficulties lie on the autistic spectrum, it is mainly intended for children whose friendship difficulties do not have an underlying medical cause. (Children who have autism will be at a lower developmental stage than other children of the same age, making the use of age-referenced activities less useful.)

The nature of friendship

What is a friend?
At different times in a child's development friends mean different things.

For the very young preschool child a friend is someone who is physically nearby. They have an egocentric view. Selman (1980) suggests the following stages.

Stage 1
This soon develops into an understanding that other people have different emotions and intentions. Friends now become anyone who shares toys with you and is kind to you.

Stage 2

By school age most children understand that friendship involves mutual respect, kindness and expressions of affection. To have a friend is to have a special kind of relationship with someone.

Stage 3

During the preadolescent phase the child is more aware of personality differences and preferences - a friend is now someone who shares similar interests and values. A friend is someone with whom you can share intimate personal information as well as receive support.

Stage 4

During adolescence friends become people who are emotionally very close to each other while respecting each other's autonomy. Friends are especially important at this time because they provide support for the adolescent's key task of becoming independent from their parents. As a result friendship difficulties can be all the more upsetting at this time.

What is clear is that children's understanding of friendships is developmental and accumulative. New understandings emerge and extend previous ones.

Why are friends important?

There are many basic needs that are met by having friends. The world is a lot less threatening when we have a friend by our side. Essentially friendship is tied up with our need to belong and to understand who we are. Our friends help us to see who we are, their reactions become the measurement of how well we think we are doing. "I see myself through your eyes." Also because friendships are built on positive emotions they help us to experience the warmth and confidence of being valued, liked, respected etc by another human being. We are, after all, social animals.

We know that children who have good friendship-making skills are more self-confident, independent and sensitive to the needs of others and are good listeners and communicators. Sadly, children who lack such skills may more often experience social isolation or rejection, are less happy and achieve less academically.

Do boys and girls differ in their friendship patterns?

Yes and no. While there are patterns, children vary a lot and we must always be sensitive to the uniqueness of any particular child. However, research has found that:

6

- Boys seem more orientated towards being part of their peer group, while girls seem to prefer pairs or smaller groups.
- The older children are, the more they seem to prefer same sex friends.
- Girls seem to use empathy as a way of resolving difficulties, while boys are more action-orientated and will use aggression.
- Girls are less inhibited in expressing a wider range of feelings.

But remember there are always exceptions - these are only patterns.

Shyness

Before looking at the different skills children require to make and stay friends, it is worth considering a more general difficulty that many children experience - shyness. If children are unsure of themselves and how to get attention they may take a passive role. If other adults and children give a lot of time and attention to them, then they may receive attention and remain shy. This may lead to them never mastering the skills of making friends or experiencing the fun of having them.

Tackling shyness
Shyness is a not uncommon difficulty for children of varying ages - in fact it is something that most of us experience at some time. The symptoms can include anxiety, feelings of sickness, a pounding heart, perspiring, blushing, shaking and believing that everyone is looking at you. All in all this can be a very unpleasant experience. The following ideas can give both the child and the adults involved suggestions to improve matters.

Children who experience shyness to the point that it prevents them making friends need to be helped to understand that shyness is an unhelpful habit they have learned, and that they can unlearn it. It can be more common during the teenage years when they become more aware of themselves as unique individuals. During this time they are thinking more about themselves than ever before and it is not surprising that this preoccupation can lead some to become very self-conscious and shyness then becomes a way of coping.

Always emphasise that shyness is a normal stage in growing up.

Establish a good relationship with the child and work with them through the following steps.

Step 1

Learn to relax. Practise tensing your muscles and then relaxing them. Start with your toes. Also breathe slowly and deeply, breathe in to the count of 7 and out to the count of 11. Short shallow breaths will make you more anxious. Internal arousal can equally be a sign that you are excited as much as frightened. Think positively, "I can cope with this", "I am in control", "Blushing is not a problem".

Step 2

Practise focusing all of your attention on what is happening around you, not inside you. Try to note all the smallest details about people you are with. Concentrate on listening very carefully to what is being said. Keep eye contact and smile. If it is your first meeting with someone try to say something even if it is, "I never know what to say when I meet people for the first time." You will be surprised as to how many will answer with, "Me neither." It may help if you act as if the other person is shy and your task is to help them.

Step 3

Take control, look for situations in which to practise your growing confidence. Remember to say to yourself, "Even if I do blush, I'm going to carry on talking - no one else is concerned." Make yourself ask questions in conversations.

Always relax, think positively, practise and reward your successes.
(Remember all confident people are shy at times.)

Friendship difficulties

While there is no simple explanation for why some children experience friendship difficulties, here are some of common ones.

- **Past experiences**
  If a child has moved to a new school and is trying to break into well-established friendship groups, they can be seen by other children as a threat. This can be especially true for girls where often "exclusive friendships" exist.
- **Skill difficulties**
  Some children may have missed out on opportunities to learn the necessary skills. They may be an only child or live in an isolated setting. The importance of turn taking and sharing may not be understood and appreciated by them.

- **Understanding and empathy**
  There are some children who have failed to learn the rules of friendship or who do not find it easy to put themselves into the "shoes" of someone else. Their behaviour can be insensitive and misunderstood by their peers who find them a threat to their own fragile sense of belonging.
- **Interaction style**
  Some children who are unsure about themselves and lack confidence may overact to compensate for this. Such children can appear to be aggressive and dominating. They consequently break some of the rules of friendship and are rejected by their peers.

Friendship skills

As children develop they learn the four cornerstones of being a friend. Two of these are internal processes - cognitive and emotional; the others are more external and behavioural - skills and role playing. While there is overlap between them, through considering them separately we can produce a model that will more readily enable us to design appropriate interventions.

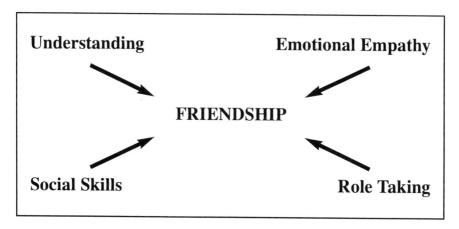

1. Social skills
Social skills refer to the range of verbal and non-verbal behaviours that are used when we relate to each other. Many, but not all, children learn these skills through observing others and practising. When they use these

9

skills they receive good feedback from people around them and happy relationships develop. However, if they use these skills inappropriately, then relationship difficulties will occur. Difficulties can be a result of either the lack of certain skills or the excessive use of them. Children who over-dominate conversations will face friendship difficulties as much as those who contribute too little.

2. Understanding

There will be some children who do not understand what it means to be a friend. It is always a good starting point to see how much a child can tell you about friends. Depending on their level of understanding you can then provide them with friendship words and what they mean as well as further information and examples.

Being a friend means:
listening, sharing, smiling, helping, caring, trusting, laughing together, spending time together.

Some	DO'S	and	DON'TS
	listen		interrupt
	share		call names
	smile		hit
	take turns		be selfish
	compliment		say nasty things

3. Emotional empathy

We have seen how important friendships are, how they develop and are maintained. A key skill in this process is the ability to empathise with each other. That is to be able to imagine the feelings that another person is experiencing and to match these to one's own. This may be a developmental problem as much as anything else. A child who lacks empathy will fail to appreciate the feelings that their behaviour may cause in another child. Such egocentric children will not be able to distinguish the emotional arousal of another child from their own. They may feel upset because another child is crying, because it is making them upset, but they do not feel sympathy for the upset child. To put it bluntly, instead of comforting the upset child, they would look for comfort for themselves. Their emotions are self-centred; if something makes them feel good, it is good, if it upsets them, it is bad. They measure all feelings against themselves, not other children.

4. Role taking

Early research thought that preschool children were not able to "put themselves into another person's shoes". But we know now that this is not so. For example, 3 year-olds will modify their speech when talking to much younger children. This can be interpreted as the emergence of an awareness of others and their needs.

From approximately 6 - 8 years of age children learn that people see things differently, but they can only manage one perspective at a time.

"I like playing football and understand that you don't."

At around 8 - 10 years children can understand how their behaviour may be seen from another person's point of view.

"When I always take my favourite sweets first you might think me selfish."

The final stage begins around 12 years when adolescents can take into account social norms and conventions as well as understanding that other people have complex but equally subjective ways of organising their world.

"Even though you like different things to me and we do not always agree, we can still be friends".

Friendship Assessment Profile

General guidelines
1. For infant-age children, focus firstly on social skills and then understanding.
2. For junior and lower secondary, improve emotional empathy before role taking.
3. Use the Friendship Record Sheet (Appendix 1) to record key information and the programme of action decided on.

Step 1
Strengths and weaknesses.
In which area/s does the child require support?

Indicative questions
When your NO answers outnumber the YES answers it indicates that this area requires development.

Understanding
1. Can they give three examples of what a friend is?
2. Do they know three ways to make a friend?
3. Can they give three ideas to help friends stay friends?
4. Can they describe how children without friends may feel?
5. Can they give three examples of why other people would like them?

Emotional empathy
1. Can they describe emotions expected in different situations, eg twisted ankle, failed test, lost money/favourite toy, argument with friend, nightmare?
2. Can they identify a range of emotions from facial expressions and body postures?
3. Can they explain why the same event can result in different emotions in different children of different ages?
4. Can they mirror other people's moods in their behaviour, voice tone etc?
5. Can they give examples as to how they would react differently to situations depending on how they felt?

Social skills
1. Can they take turns, in conversations and waiting to be served in queue?
2. Do they greet people appropriately, friends they know and people they don't?
3. Do they offer help appropriately, for example when people are stuck with a problem as compared to when they have lost something?
4. Do they listen and remember what is said to them?
5. Can they share possessions?

Role taking
1. Can they explain how their behaviour may affect others?
2. Can they tell a story from another person's viewpoint?
3. Can they understand that different people may see the same event differently?
4. Are they able to describe the kind of support children might need in different circumstances? (For example, problem with homework, being teased, 3 year-old separated from parents?)
5. Can they describe how they would act if they were a famous singer, a lost child, a victim of bullying?

Many children will have difficulties in a number of areas.

Using your knowledge of the child, choose the area where you believe they are most likely to experience success.

Step 2

The following Tool Box is not exhaustive but will provide you with examples of the kind of interventions that would most appropriately improve a specific area, as well as guidelines.

The Friendship Tool Box

Developing social skills

1. Discuss with the child the advantages and disadvantages of having certain skills.
2. Focus on the skill and model it for them. Let them watch videos to see the skill in use. (For example, skills such as waiting for a pause in the conversation before speaking.)
3. Allow them to rehearse it and to imagine themselves doing it. Talk them through it.
4. Give them precise feedback as to how they are doing. Explain how other people may react and if appropriate show them. Make sure it is a small achievable skill.
5. With the child explore situations where they can begin to practise, and practise the skill.
6. Play board games to teach them the importance of following agreed rules.
7. Allow the child opportunities to both share something of theirs with other children and to share something belonging to others. Talk through the benefits afterwards.
8. Discuss the role and importance of saying, "please", "thank you" and "excuse me", and show your appreciation when they use them.
9. Use comics, picture books and ask the child to predict what key characters will do next.
10. If there is an appropriate media role model that the child likes, watch them on video and discuss their behaviour, popularity etc.

Developing understanding

1. Help the child to keep a diary of key actions that they do that support friendship, such as sharing, helping, spending time together.
2. The child produces their own record of "What a friend is". Examples are included of how to make a friend and keep friends.
3. The child discusses with an adult how certain actions lead to positive feelings and others (such as name calling) to hurtful ones.

4. A profile of the child's interests, skills and qualities is made which helps them to be a friend.
5. Past examples of when they were friendly are recalled, recorded and looked at in detail.
6. Create word searches with key concepts - appropriate for the child's understanding - to do with friendship. (For example, share, care, help, like, together, support, play, trust, loyalty, fun, interests, talk, take turns, etc. See Appendix 2.)
7. Set the child a task of coming up with three ways to help an alien, called "Al", to make friends when they arrive on earth. (Or a new pupil in school.)
8. Make a collage of pictures that reflect children and people being friendly.
9. Support the child in having a pen-friend in another local school, or different part of the country. (See reference WRITE AWAY.)
10. Discuss with the child who they would like to be friends with. Discuss ideas and short-term targets that would help achieve this goal.

Developing emotional empathy
1. Use comics and books to help children recognise different emotions from the facial and physical cues.
2. Make up stories about people and events and keep checking if the child can predict the feelings different characters will have.
3. Develop character cards of children facing different challenges and see if the child can explain the feelings they will have and why. (For example, child at dentist's, child unwrapping present, child separated from parents.)
4. Establish that the child has a range of feeling words and understands situations that give rise to them.
5. Can the child explain why the same situation could give rise to different emotions in different people?
6. Ask them to make up stories about children in different situations. What feelings will they have in the different situations?
7. Use puppets to act out situations and keep stopping to ask the child what they are feeling inside.
8. Develop a "feeling thermometer 1 - 10". Establish a range of words to describe different points. (Perhaps 1 is terrible and 10 is fantastic.) Each day discuss where they and you are and why.
9. Develop word searches for feeling words and do anagrams as well. (See Appendix 2.)
10. Play a game with the child guessing your feelings from facial expressions, body posture, tone of voice.

Role taking

1. Set up imaginary situations and then ask the child to act out a part. Ask them to step out of the part and explain what they are thinking as the character.
2. Using stories, ask them to put themselves into the shoes of the characters. "What would they do if they were the character?"
3. Let them observe role plays and then talk about what would happen if a key skill had not been used.
4. Set other children up with roles and the focus child tells them how to act.
5. Set homework tasks where the child has to practise a specific skill each week.
6. Teach the child the necessary skills to act "as if" they had certain qualities. (For example, to be happy, sad, angry.)
7. Play "mirroring", where the child copies all the mannerisms etc of someone else, and then works out what that person was thinking and feeling.
8. What happened next. Write cards with a range of situations on them, "Child gets pushed out of dinner queue." "Child wrongly accused of breaking a rule."
9. Help the child to write a "mini-play" with several characters. How would they act out the different parts?
10. Make up the beginning of a story with several characters and then help the child to write different endings for the characters.

While we have so far looked at ways of developing individual support programmes to enable children to develop friendships there is an approach that enlists the support of other children to achieve the same end. There will be times when a friendless child will behave aggressively towards peers. Their unpredictability will understandably lead to peers avoiding them. This in turn can lead to an increase in negative behaviour. A positive way to develop friendships for such children is to use a "Circle of friends".

Circle of Friends

Including children with emotional and behavioural difficulties

This approach was developed in Canada as a means to support the active inclusion of pupils with various challenges. The ideas presented below are drawn from its practical application as reported by Newton and Wilson (1996). They used it to promote the inclusion of a pupil with emotional and behavioural difficulties. School staff are well aware of new initiatives which are promoted as "catch-all" solutions. A Circle of Friends approach needs to be approached cautiously, we do not always control all the factors to ensure success. Nevertheless it is a contribution worth our consideration, and there may well be useful ideas within it.

Circle of Friends is a powerful tool to enable all children to appreciate - from the heart - the importance of having friends. But it is unlikely to be the solution for every friendship difficulty. There may be aspects of it which are helpful. Try to pilot a circle before applying it, to iron out snags and to develop the necessary resources and skills. Then you will be better prepared to tackle more challenging circumstances.

Setting the scene
Explain the approach to the focus child's parents or carers. In basic terms explain to the focus child the aims of setting up a Circle of Friends. The chosen circle will offer them support and ideas to help them enjoy school more.

Meeting the class
Someone new to the class can increase the perceived importance of the project by the children. Aims of the session:

a) Confidentiality - the focus child has given permission to talk about themselves, but what goes on in this session is private.
b) Focus child's behaviour, positives and negatives. Children are reminded that the more honest they are the more helpful they can be. It can be worth emphasising that it is the behaviour not the child that is causing concern. A list (1) is made of negatives.

Understanding friendship
Children are asked to draw a circle and:

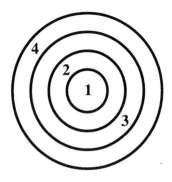

- In the innermost one place those that are closest to them, their family. (1)
- Then in the next circle they put their closest friends. (2)
- The next circle contains acquaintances, people they meet but do not know all that well. (3)
- The outer circle contains people that are known because they are paid to be in their life, teachers for example. (4)

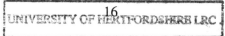

- The group is now asked to describe how they think they would feel if they only had people in the first and fourth circles, no friends or acquaintances.

Typical responses are:

lonely, scared, frightened, angry, fed up, sad.

They are then asked how they think they would behave and a list is made (List 2).

Again some examples are:

run away, swear, throw things at people, shout, hit people.

List comparison
List 1 and List 2 are now compared and it becomes clear that some of the behaviours are similar. The discussion can now be around the possibility that some of the focus child's problem behaviour may be, in part, a result of not having friends. If you think you are not liked and rejected then you are likely to be aggressive.

What do we do that doesn't help?
The class can now pool examples of things that they perceive do not help the focus child feel that they belong to the group. (For example, being teased, left out of games etc.) The aim is not to blame anyone but to understand that there will be situations that the focus child finds difficult.

What do we do that helps?
The group can now pool ideas as to what could be done by them to help include the focus child.

Setting up a Circle of Friends
It is made easier at this point if sooner or later everyone will have the opportunity to be a Friend. A small group of some six to eight is chosen to put some of the suggestions into action. Children who themselves have emotional and behavioural difficulties can be excellent befrienders, therefore exclude no one. Those not chosen this time can be reminded that even though they are not in the inner circle this time they can still be helpful and supportive.

It is important to emphasise that those chosen to be part of a Circle of Friends will only do so for a fixed and short period. This removes any child's apprehension about always having to be a friend to someone. It can also mean that when they are no longer in the Circle of Friends there is an increased possibility that they will befriend the focus child through choice.

Support and monitor
Soon after this a meeting should be held with the Circle of Friends and the focus child to see what progress has been made. Further meetings will need to be arranged and the adult facilitator will not only enhance the group's effectiveness through encouraging problem solving activities but also provide praise and recognition for the efforts and progress made by all.

Through increasing our understanding of how children develop friendships and the skills necessary for this we can design programmes that go beyond our everyday understanding. This booklet has highlighted the core skills needed and strategies for when they are underdeveloped. Having and being a friend enables children to experience a wide range of positive emotions and all should be included.

APPENDIX 1

FRIENDSHIP RECORD SHEET

Pupil's Name: ....

Date of Birth: ....

Year Group:...

Outline of Concern: ....

....

Friendship Assessment Indicators

Understanding..

Empathy...

Role Taking...

Social Skills ....

Contact with home made by: ....

....

Date..

Outcome: ....

....

Agreed Target/s

1. ....

2. ....

Interventions

....

....

....

....

....

....

Success Indicators

....

....

....

....

....

Review Date..

HOW MANY WORDS TO DO WITH FRIENDSHIP CAN YOU FIND?

```
L  F  U  N  J  U  O  T  R  D  C  X  S  J  O  I  N
L  I  K  E  R  T  Y  U  I  O  P  E  Q  U  A  L  F
D  S  H  A  R  E  V  B  N  M  H  E  L  P  W  M  S
C  D  E  R  F  V  B  G  T  Y  H  N  M  J  U  I  D
L  T  O  G  E  T  H  E  R  L  I  S  T  E  N  C  T
K  L  P  T  A  L  K  T  R  M  A  T  E  R  G  H  E
L  O  Q  A  Z  X  S  W  C  O  N  T  A  C  T  B  G
H  C  L  O  S  E  N  E  S  S  Y  T  C  A  R  E  K
E  L  P  Y  T  R  E  X  S  H  A  R  E  Y  T  R  D
G  H  J  K  N  B  V  F  D  S  W  R  E  P  A  L  B
L  M  A  T  E  U  O  T  B  U  D  D  Y  Z  B  N  U
R  A  P  P  O  R  T  Y  T  S  U  P  P  O  R  T  Q
H  K  L  I  N  K  Z  X  E  X  C  H  A  N  G  E  J
P  A  R  T  N  E  R  S  H  I  P  O  L  J  H  M  D
```

CAN YOU UNSCRAMBLE THESE FRIENDSHIP WORDS?

1.   T H E T G O R E

    _ _ _ _ _ _ _ _

2.   M O N U M T C I A O C I N

    _ _ _ _ _ _ _ _ _ _ _ _ _

3.   N F U

    _ _ _

References

Erwin, P. (1993) *Friendship and Peer Relations in Children.* Wiley: Chichester.

Newton, C. & Wilson, D. (1996) 'Circles of Friends' in *Educational Psychology in Practice*, Vol. 11, No. 4, January 1996.

O'Rourke, K. & Worzbyt, J. (1996) *Support Groups for Children.* Accelerated Development: Washington.

Selman, R. (1980) *The Growth of Interpersonal Understanding.* Academic Press: New York.

WRITE AWAY, 1 Thorpe Close, London W10 5XL.